Bedtime Fun Book

Anne Ingram and Peggy O'Donnell

Illustrations by Dee Huxley

HAMLYN

For H & B
who have tried them all

Contents

It's Fun Going to Bed

Going to bed is important, because sleep is necessary. In fact, experts say we can die quicker from lack of sleep than we can from lack of food!

Another point to remember is that we spend a third of our lives sleeping. That works out at 121 days every year or, if we live to be 75 years old, we will have spent 25 of those years sleeping.

So let's make the most of the time we are awake! And, it always happens — just when you're right in the middle of a great game or doing something really interesting, there will be a call from somewhere: "Time for bed!"

This book is chock-a-block full of reasons for going to bed early, that is, *before* that call comes, and spending the time doing fun things in your bedroom. You never know your luck, once you are there the adults might think you have gone to sleep and forget to check — it's worth a try.

6

There are great ideas of things to do if you're alone, or things to do if you are sharing your room with family or friends.

Remember though — sleep is important, so we have included a tip (on the last page of the book) for those nights when you are having trouble settling down.

Your bed is an essential part of your life — you'd be very uncomfortable without one! It's certainly the most used piece of furniture in the house, and it's probably the one most taken for granted by all of us. But the bed has had a fascinating history and several people have invented some weird ones (see page 10).

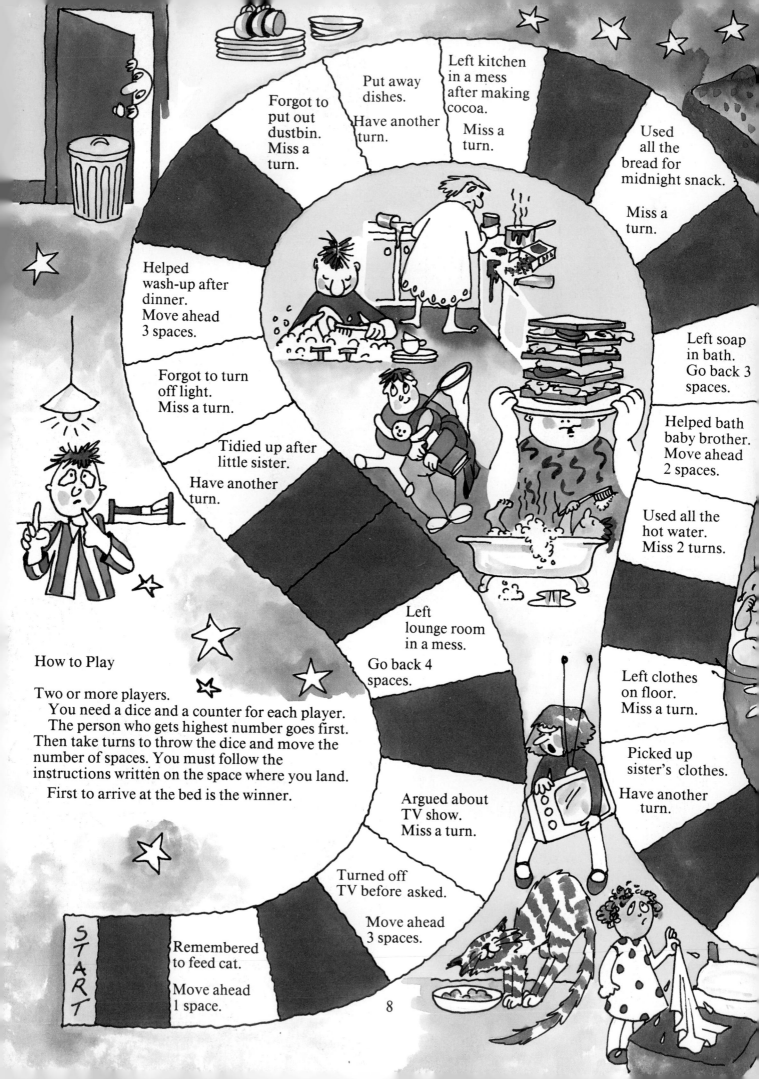

Forgot to put out dustbin. Miss a turn.

Put away dishes. Have another turn.

Left kitchen in a mess after making cocoa. Miss a turn.

Used all the bread for midnight snack. Miss a turn.

Helped wash-up after dinner. Move ahead 3 spaces.

Left soap in bath. Go back 3 spaces.

Forgot to turn off light. Miss a turn.

Helped bath baby brother. Move ahead 2 spaces.

Tidied up after little sister. Have another turn.

Used all the hot water. Miss 2 turns.

Left lounge room in a mess. Go back 4 spaces.

Left clothes on floor. Miss a turn.

Picked up sister's clothes. Have another turn.

Argued about TV show. Miss a turn.

How to Play

Two or more players.
  You need a dice and a counter for each player.
  The person who gets highest number goes first.
Then take turns to throw the dice and move the number of spaces. You must follow the instructions written on the space where you land.

  First to arrive at the bed is the winner.

Turned off TV before asked. Move ahead 3 spaces.

Remembered to feed cat. Move ahead 1 space.

START

8

Took cat to bed. Miss 2 turns.

Covers fall off bed. Miss a turn.

Turned out light when told. Have another turn.

Didn't put toys away. Go back 6 spaces.

Tidied up bedroom. Have another turn.

Forgot to clean teeth. Move back 4 spaces.

Read till late at night. Miss 2 turns.

Helped remake brother's bed. Move ahead 2 spaces.

Short sheeted brother's bed. Move back 2 spaces.

Bedroom in mess. Throw 6 to finish.

FINISH

Built den in bed. Move ahead 2 spaces.

Forgot to return pillows. Miss a turn.

Remade bed. Move ahead 1 space.

Frightened brother with ghost story. Miss a turn.

Mosquitoes in bedroom. Move back 2 spaces.

Forgot to tuck-in sister's bed. Miss a turn.

Remembered to turn off kitchen light. Move ahead 2 spaces.

Forgot to give sister a drink. Move back 2 spaces.

Locked cat in bathroom. Move back 4 spaces.

Found teddy in garden. Have another turn.

Can't find baby brother's teddy bear. Miss a turn.

owel d. a

Dressed sister. Move ahead 1 space.

Read sister story. Move ahead 2 spaces.

Tied knot in sister's pyjamas. Go back 2 spaces.

Bed Trivia

The history of the bed

The first bed was probably just a pile of leaves scraped together to make the ground softer. Next came a stone or wooden bench on which was placed a sack that had been filled with straw, to make a mattress. The skin of an animal was used as a blanket.

It is recorded that during the third century one of the emperors of Rome had his bed made of solid silver.

During the Middle Ages, benches were given up as the place to sleep and frames were built to hold the mattresses. By the thirteenth century people began to hang canopies from the ceilings which came down over their beds. This led to the practice of hanging curtains around all four sides of the bed for warmth and privacy.

In England, during the sixteenth century, a giant bed was built for a very large family — it was 3 x 3.3 metres! And they all slept in it together!

Today beds come in every shape and size — round beds, waterbeds, motorised beds, even suspension beds.

Did you know?

- King Louis of France had 413 beds.
- "Goodnight" was the last word spoken by the nineteenth century romantic poet, Lord Byron, before he died.
- Catherine the Great, Winston Churchill and Napoleon Bonaparte, all suffered from insomnia.

- The ancient Egyptians must have had difficulty going to sleep — they used pillows made of stone!
- Your bed will last, on the average, about fourteen years. This means that most people will wear out five beds during their life.

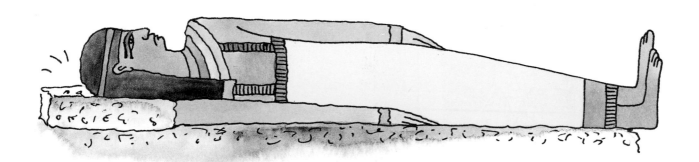

"Bed" has many meanings

Bed is a busy word. It is used in many ways to describe various things. Here are a few:

- a plot of ground in which plants are grown is a flower bed
- the bottom of a river or a lake is called the bed
- a layer of crushed rock, used as the foundation for a railway track or a road, is also a bed
- the flesh around an animal's claw is referred to as the bed
- a bed bug is a small blood-sucking insect

- a bed chamber is an old-fashioned word for bedroom
- when travelling you will often see a sign 'B & B' (this is a house offering Bed and Breakfast for travellers)
- a bed warmer is a metal pan containing hot coals and was used in the days before hot water bottles or electric blankets

- a bed roll is a portable bed, such as a sleeping bag which you take camping
- a bed of roses means everything is very comfortable
- to get out of bed on the wrong side means you'll be in a bad mood all day.

Body Tricks

We all take our bodies for granted and we never really know all that they can do. Here are a few fun tricks to try out in your bedroom, before you try them on your friends. You will be surprised at how your body reacts.

Floating arms

Stand in your bedroom doorway with the backs of your hands pressed firmly against the door jamb (as shown). Press hard, as if you are trying to lift your arms above your head. Keep pressing while you slowly count off 60 seconds. Now walk away with your hands down. They won't stay down for long, they will begin to move upwards without you doing a thing.

Stork stance

Stand on one foot and shut your eyes tightly, they must remain shut the whole time. Now, keeping that same foot off the ground, slowly begin to count to 50 — you probably won't make it because it is almost impossible to keep your balance with your eyes closed. Keep trying.

Moving arrows

Take a sheet of white paper and draw an arrow (like this one) filling it in well. Prop it up on the desk in your bedroom. Fill a clear glass with water and place it in front of the arrow. Now stand a little way back with your eyes at the same level as the glass. Watch as the arrow changes direction.

Wobbly knees

Find a section of wall in your bedroom that is clear of things. Stand sideways against the wall pressing your shoulder, arm, elbow, leg and foot firmly against it. Now try and lift your other foot — you'll find you have a problem.

Knee walking

Let's see how fit you are. Sit cross-legged on the floor and bring your feet up to rest on your knees — this will take a little practice. Once you have mastered this, rock yourself forward so that you are balancing on your knees. Keeping your hands off the ground try and walk on your knees — it's not easy.

Toe touching

Go back to that clear section of wall. Stand up straight with your back against it. Now bend forward and touch your toes, keeping your knees straight. It's a good idea to have a pillow, or something soft in front of you, because you are going to be falling forward.

Jokes and Puzzles

Q. Why is the letter "e" lazy?
A. Because it's always in bed.

Q. What turned the moon pale?
A. At-mos-fear.

Q. Why did the girl go to sleep in the fire-place?
A. Because she wanted to sleep like a log.

Q. Why did the burglar cut the legs off his bed?
A. Because he wanted to lie low for a while.

Q. What does a cat sleep on?
A. A caterpillar.

Q. What does a Scotsman sleep under?
A. A continental kilt.

Q. What is the difference between a night watchman and a butcher?
A. One stays awake and the other weighs the steak.

Jigword

To find the missing word, write the names of the objects in the picture and cross out the unwanted letters.

Make up your own Jigword puzzles based on the things in your bedroom. Draw your own clues and try them out on your friends.

(Answer: Bedroom)

14

Picture puzzle

The pictures below show a typical bedroom shared by three children. Although these two pictures look exactly the same, there are ten differences between them. Can you find them?

(Answer: Keep looking till you find them)

15

Den Beds

Turn your bed into your own private den, or
boat, or train, or whatever you fancy.

All you need is your bed, the bed covers
and as many pillows as you can find.

Now go to it — and have fun.

Remember to return everything you borrowed from other people's beds. Also, remake your own bed before settling down.

Playing with Shadows

Games with shadows are great fun. You can use a torch, your bed lamp or the overhead light; it all depends on the type and size of the shadow you want to make, or on the game you are playing.

Shadows can be made with your hands or with your whole body. You can also use your toys to be characters in your own shadow puppet theatre.

Hand shadows

These are best made when sitting up in bed. You will need a plain wall on one side and a torch or bed lamp on the other.

Now try these:

Rabbit	Snake
Bird	Elephant
Dog	Duck
Crocodile	

Try making the shadows with both hands and, when you become an expert, you can make the duck talk to the crocodile.

18

Body shadows

You make these when you are out of bed and have the overhead light on, but you will need to have a clear floor space in front of you.

Try these:
Monster
Headless person

Another idea is to draw your own portrait, but you will need a friend to help you. Spread out a large sheet of paper (lining paper is quite good). Stand with the light behind you and your shadow on the paper. Have your hands on your hips and your legs slightly apart. Now ask your friend to draw around the outside of your shadow using a pencil or crayon.

Later on you can colour in this portrait, marking in your clothes, and give it to your family as a present.

Shadow puppets

If you have a couple of friends to stay you can make up your own shadow puppet play, build a theatre, and use your toys as the characters.

Move your bed against the wall (this wall needs to be clear of posters and things), with a bed lamp set-up on a chair or desk behind you.

The idea is for you and your friends to sit on the floor, below the level of the light, and to move your characters along the bed, which has become the stage.

From where you sit you can watch your shadow play happening on the wall while moving your puppets and speaking their parts. It's fun to use the hand shadows as well.

19

Optical Illusions

An optical illusion is something that looks like one thing, but it really isn't that way at all. What is happening is that your brain is receiving information which becomes confused when certain combinations of lines are used together.

For example, look at these two horizontal lines. Which is the longer?

A ruler will show you that they are both exactly the same length, although your brain will have told you that the bottom one is the longer. This is caused by the angle of the arrows used at the ends of the lines.

It's interesting to know that this puzzle was first devised in 1889 by a German psychiatrist. The next two were also devised by Germans, one in 1860, the other in 1861. See if you can solve them:

No 1 In which box are all the long lines parallel?

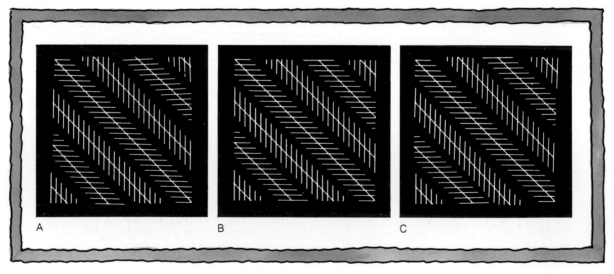

No 2 In which illustration are the long horizontal lines parallel?

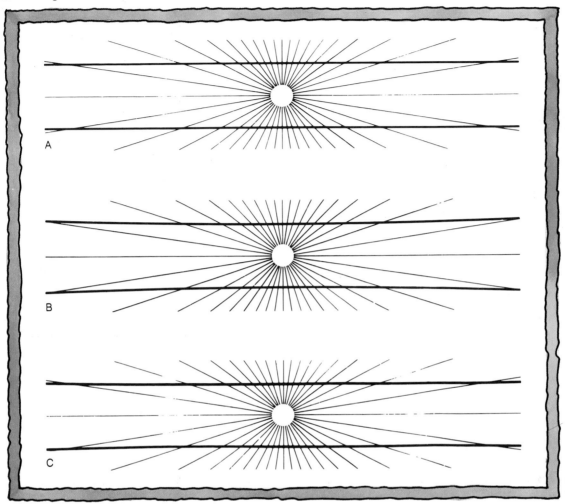

These next two optical illusions are slightly different. If you look at them for too long you'll begin to wonder if you're going crazy!

The impossible triangle

The weird prongs

Now try and draw them. Then make up your own optical illusion.

(Answers: 1b, 2a)

21

Become a Magician

Your bedroom is the ideal place to practise magic tricks and become expert enough to put on a magic show for your family and friends.

Every magician needs a magic wand. It's very useful to wave in the air as you say your magic words or, better still, it can be used to point out things which then distract the audience while you are doing the secret part of the trick.

It's very simple to make a wand. All you need is a length of dowel, about 30 or 40cm, which should then be painted black — except for its magic tips which can be white or yellow or blue.

Set yourself up in your bedroom, in front of a mirror, and start practising. This way you can see all your mistakes and correct them.

Begin with the following few tricks then, next time you are at your local library, borrow a couple of books on magic and learn some more.

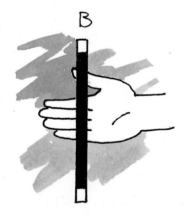

Magic wand trick

You will need:
your magic wand
a pin

How to perform:
Make this the first trick you do for your audience. Before the curtain rises, push the pin into the side of your magic wand — about half-way down.

Now tell your audience that you have a magic wand that sticks to your hand when you instruct it. (Follow diagrams). Remember to secretly slip out the pin before beginning your next trick.

Magic matchbox

You will need:
2 boxes of used matches (same brand)
glue

How to make:
Cut the top off one box and paste it onto the other, so that each side is the same. Onto the back of the tray that holds the matches, paste a line of matches, so that it looks like a full tray. Fill the tray with matches.

How to perform:
Show your audience the full box of matches. Close the box, rattle it, then open and tip all the matches onto the floor. Close the box, carefully turning it over in your hand. Wave your magic wand and — hey presto! a full box of matches.

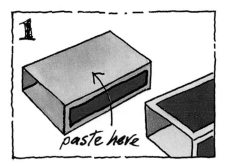

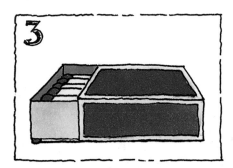

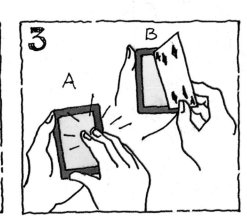

Magic cards

You will need:
a pack of cards

How to perform:
Hold the pack of cards in one hand. Carefully pick the top two cards off the pack, holding them together so that it looks like one card only, while telling your audience that you are taking off one card. Show the audience the card. (Follow diagrams).

Place both cards back on the pack. Put the top card on the bottom of the pack, letting everyone see you doing this. Give the pack of cards a couple of taps with your wand and there is your card on the top of the pack again.

Secret Codes and Messages

If you sneak up to your bedroom early, without letting anyone see you, you will be able to work on your secret codes and write private messages to your friends.

Invisible writing

Invisible ink is the ideal way to send a secret message. Write your message on an old letter you have received using the white spaces between the lines for your invisible writing.

Invisible inks can be made from a variety of ingredients:

- lemon juice
- milk
- sugar and water
- potato juice

To write your message always use the wrong end of a used match and remember to print, don't use running writing. As the "ink" dries it becomes invisible; however, your friend will be able to read it by warming it on a light bulb, or pressing it with an iron on the lowest heat.

Scrambler stick

You and your friend will need pencils that are exactly the same size — in both width and length — then you will be able to send secret messages.

Cut a length of paper, about 5mm wide. Tape one end to the top of the pencil, then carefully wind the paper around the pencil (as shown). Tape down bottom end.

Now put a dot where your message begins. Print your message along the pencil (as shown). When you have finished carefully unwind the paper. Your message is now all jumbled up and can only be read by your friend when it has been wound around the pencil that matches yours.

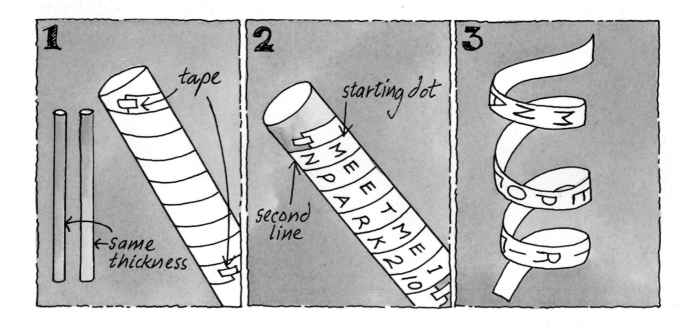

Coded messages

There are hundreds of codes that have been invented over the years and used in all kinds of secret operations. Some people keep their diaries in code so that no one can read them.

The best code of all is the one you invent yourself. This you can do by using a jumble of letters and numbers. For example, choose a key word, like ORANGE (your key word must not have a repeat of any letter in it, so APPLE would not do).

Using the simple system of making each letter a number, your code would work like this:

O	R	A	N	G	E	B	C
1	2	3	4	5	6	7	8
D	F	H	I	J	K	L	M
9	10	11	12	13	14	15	16
P	Q	S	T	U	V	W	X
17	18	19	20	21	22	23	24
Y	Z						
25	26						

Work out this message

```
16   6   6   20
12   4       1  21  2
 8  21   7   7  25
 3  20      4PM
```

By using a key word you confuse anyone trying to break your code. If you used a simple code, such as A=1, B=2, C=3 and so on, it would be very easy for someone to break it and read your secret message.

If you want to try breaking a really difficult code, borrow a copy of the book *Red Shift* by Alan Garner, from your library.

Messages through the Night

This won't work. The string must be tight.

If you have a good friend living next door, it is possible to talk to each other every night without leaving your bedrooms or using the family telephone. What you do is make your own private telephone.

String telephone

This can work very well so long as the string remains taut and you can keep it well out of everyone's way, so it's best to do this only if both you and your friend have upstairs bedrooms.

You will need:
  2 empty tins
  a ball of string
  2 used matchsticks
  hammer and large nail

How to make:
First you will need to measure the amount of string required to stretch between your two bedrooms. Cut this off, allowing an extra 200mm each end.

Wash the tins thoroughly, otherwise you'll end up with sticky ears! Also remove the labels. With the hammer and nail punch a hole in the centre of the bottom of each tin.

Thread one end of the string through the hole in the first tin, making it firm by tying it around one of the match sticks (attach with a figure eight knot as shown on page 46). Then take the string out through a ground floor window and in through your friend's ground floor window. Tie to the second tin as before.

Your private phone is now ready to use.

Messages by torch

If you are unable to rig up a string telephone, don't worry, there are other ways of making contact with your friends at night.

All you need is a torch each, plus a copy of the Morse Code alphabet. Now you are ready to send your message.

Morse Code is very useful to know. If you want to send private messages at school you can always blink your eyes, or tap the desk (not too loudly!).

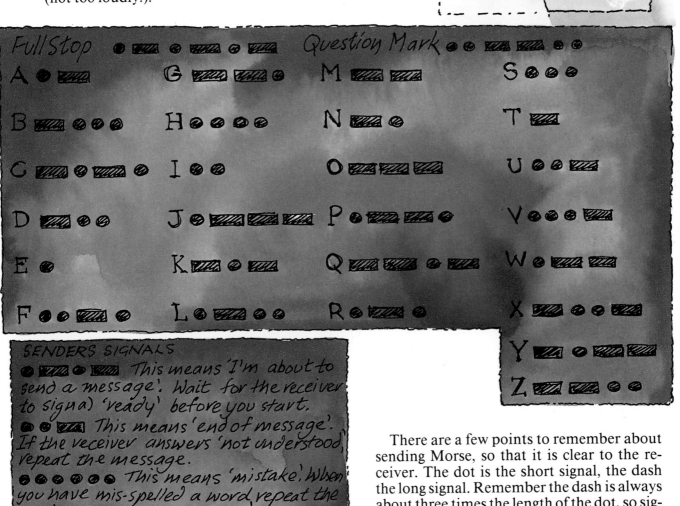

There are a few points to remember about sending Morse, so that it is clear to the receiver. The dot is the short signal, the dash the long signal. Remember the dash is always about three times the length of the dot, so signal carefully. For example, when using your torch, count to one as you flash a dot, and count to three as you flash the dash. Don't run your words or letters together, again allow a space. Count to three between letters and to five between words.

We have included these extra signals so that you will be sure your friend is receiving you.

Spy Stoppers

When you need time alone to work out a secret code, or send a torch message to your friend across the street, you need to be sure that no one will sneak into your bedroom unannounced. So build yourself an alarm system that will alert you when the door is opened — it will also frighten the person who opened it!

Door alarm

Make this during the day so that you have it ready to set up when you go to your bedroom.

You will need:
 an empty matchbox
 sticky tape
 30cm length of cotton
 dried peas or small stones

How to make:
Take the inside tray out of the matchbox, cut off one end and slip the tray back inside. Now firmly tape the sealed end so that you make a small box (as shown). Fill the box with the dried peas or small stones.

 Tape one end of the cotton to the matchbox, then carefully prop this up on the door frame (as shown). Tape the other end of the cotton to the door. Now, when the door is opened, hey presto, dried peas everywhere and lots of noise!

tape

thread

There are always times when you need to leave something secret or important in your bedroom, but you need to know whether anyone has looked at it while you were out. Here are a couple of traps you can set up to keep tabs on everything:

Paper trap

Leave a few unimportant papers scattered on the top of your desk, slightly messy, along with a pencil and other odds and ends. Draw a fine line across two of the papers (as shown). When you come back you will be able to tell whether anyone has touched them.

Secret-drawer trap

All you need to set this trap up is a hair pulled from your head. Using two small pieces of sticky tape, you tape both ends of the hair down one on either side of the opening crack of the drawer (as shown). This way you will know when your secret drawer has been opened in your absence.

This trap can be used on anything that opens, like doors, windows, books — it's easy and very effective.

Sky Watch

Sky watching is a great pastime. Turn out all the lights in your bedrooom, take a chair over to your window, make yourself comfortable and let your eyes adjust to the outside night world. You'll be surprised at what you will see.

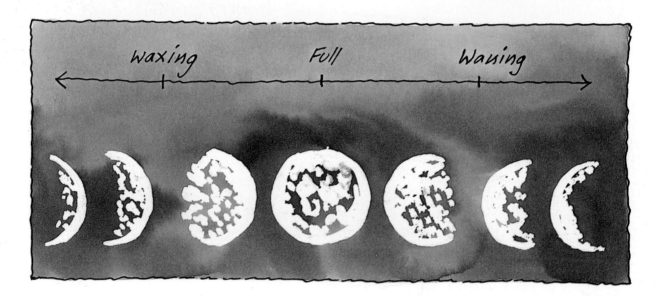

Sky trivia

Astronomers estimate that there could be up to 10 million black holes in the Milky Way Galaxy.

Cosmic rays are ultra high speed atomic particles that come shooting to earth from outer space.

Stars are not just scattered around the universe, they are grouped in great clouds or galaxies, each of which contains thousands of millions of stars.

Constellation is the name given to groups of stars that seem to make a particular shape or pattern in the sky.

A "light year" is the term given to the distance light travels in one year, which is 9,460,000 million kilometres.

Earth's nearest neighbour

These are the phases of the moon as we see them from our planet. It takes 29½ days for the moon to complete its full cycle.

The waxing moon is the one that grows larger and brighter until it becomes a full moon. Then it begins to wane and grow smaller until it disappears — this is when it lies completely in the sun's shadow.

Sky puzzle

Here is a list of the ten brightest stars in the sky and their constellations. How many can you see from your bedroom window? Borrow a book on the stars from your library to help you. Remember, if you live south of the equator you will see different ones to someone living in the northern hemisphere.

Name	Constellation
Sirius	Canis Major
Canopus	Carina
Alpha Centauri	Centaurus
Arcturus	Bootes
Vega	Lyra
Capella	Auriga
Rigel	Orion
Procyon	Canis Major
Achernar	Eridanus
Beta Centauri	Centaurus

Flying objects

These could be anything from bats to insects to satellites, all of which inhabit our night skies, so keep your eyes open for them.

Shooting stars

You will often see shooting stars at night. These are really meteors made up of debris left by the comets. Meteors can be as tiny as a pinhead and around 100 million of them hurtle into our atmosphere every day, at speeds up to 70 kilometres a second.

About 80 kilometres above the earth they burn up and disintegrate and it is this that produces the streaks of light we call shooting stars.

Apple Pie Beds

It's fun to play a trick on someone in your family, but remember not to do the same tricks too often or it won't surprise them any more.

You will need to slip away from the family when they are all busy, so the best time is usually when everyone is watching television — they won't even notice you've gone.

Decide whose bed you are going to attack, then slip quietly into their bedroom. Here's a few ideas as to what you can do.

Short-sheeting

To short-sheet your victim's bed you will need the time to totally remake it. Pull back everything, except for the bottom sheet. Go to the foot of the bed, untuck that end of the bottom sheet and bring it up to the top of the bed.

Your next job is to hide the top sheet and the best way to do this is to fold it flat at the end of the bed. Now you bring up the blankets, which cover the top sheet. Use the top half of the bottom sheet as if it was the real top sheet, turning it back on the blankets (as shown). Remember to tuck in the sides.

When your victim comes to bed they will hop in and wonder why their feet don't reach the bottom. It will take them a few minutes to work out what has happened and, because they are going to have to remake their bed before going to sleep, it's a good idea if you pretend to be asleep!

Bumpy beds

Another simple trick that's easy to do is the bumpy bed or bumpy pillow one. All that's needed is something hidden, either under the bottom sheet or in the pillow case. A plastic cooking spoon is very effective for this trick, because it's flat and rather uncomfortable when someone lies on it.

Remember to smooth out your victim's bed after you have planted something in it, then they won't be suspicious.

Knotted pyjamas

This is great fun and far less trouble than short sheeting. All you have to do is take your victim's pyjamas and tie a knot either in one of the legs or an arm. Just a single, overhand knot will do, but pull it tight!

Again, keep well away from the scene when your victim is trying to put the pyjamas on.

Bedroom Games

Here are a few games that can be played in your bedroom when you have friends staying. They are fairly quiet games so that you won't disturb anyone.

What am I doing?

You don't need any props for this game, just a good imagination. It can be played with any number of players.

One player is chosen to be "the actor" and thinks up a "what am I doing?" idea, which is then acted out for the other players who fire questions at the actor, trying to guess what is happening. The questions go on until the right answer is given, or everyone gives in.

For example, the actor could mime washing an elephant. Remember that the more way-out the occupation the harder it will be for the players to guess. A few other ideas are:

- What am I doing? Planting a tree!
- What am I doing? Cooking a cat!

And so on. It is all great fun.

Boxed in

For this game you will need a pencil for each player and a sheet of paper. It can be played by two or more players.

Mark out a square with dots (as shown), seven by seven is a good size to begin. Each player takes a turn at joining two dots together by drawing either a horizontal or vertical line (as shown).

The idea is to complete a square (or box), but not to let the other players do this. When a box is completed the player puts their initials in it and has another turn, until no more boxes can be completed. The winner is the player who has initialled the most boxes.

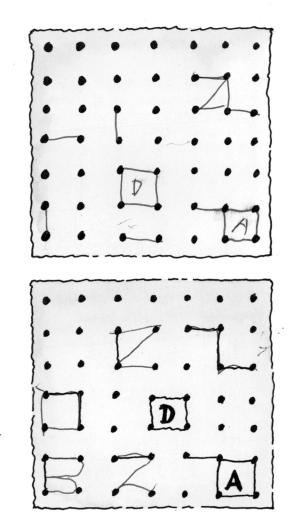

Word tennis

All you need for this game is a good memory. It is played by two players at a time, with a third player acting as umpire.

The umpire gives the two tennis players a subject, for example: cars.

Now the game begins. The first player says "Ford", the second player replies with "Rolls Royce" (the reply has to be given within three seconds and the umpire's decision is final). The players battle backwards and forwards with words until one of them either repeats a word or cannot think of one, thus losing the game. The winner then challenges a new player. And so on.

35

Sleepy Facts

Every living thing — people, animals, birds even plants — needs a period of rest. It varies as to how much each one needs, when they need it and how they get it. Here are a few fascinating facts about sleep:

Families of sea otters that feed in the kelp beds (which is a forest of seaweed) off the coast of California, seldom come ashore — they even sleep at sea. To do this they wrap themselves up in the strands of kelp which act as an anchor. It also keeps the families together. They can then go to sleep and the fast-moving currents can't sweep them away.

The blood-sucking vampire bat strikes at night when its victim is asleep. It settles on a large animal, such as a cow, then makes a shallow bite (which doesn't wake the animal). Blood runs from the wound and the bat laps it up.

Lung fish will sleep, sometimes for years, to escape death when their pond dries up. They bury themselves in the mud and wait for the rains to come and awaken them.

awake

The Fusilier fish changes colour as it goes to sleep. During the day it is a light blue as it feeds on the sunny surface of the water. At night, it sleeps on the sea bed which is dark blue and red, so it changes its colours to match its background. A great camouflage trick.

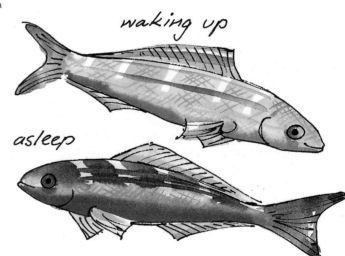

waking up

asleep

Every night you grow about 8 mm while you are asleep, but you shrink back to your former height the following day.

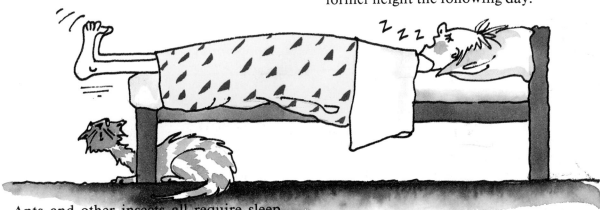

Ants and other insects all require sleep. They find a small depression in the soil which they use as a bed, lying down and pulling their legs close into their body. When they wake up they look almost human. They stretch their six legs out, often shaking them, then open their jaws as if yawning.

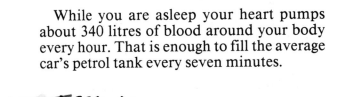

While you are asleep your heart pumps about 340 litres of blood around your body every hour. That is enough to fill the average car's petrol tank every seven minutes.

The Mojave squirrel of North America survives the long winter droughts by sleeping for at least five days a week. It sleeps in a burrow about a metre underground and this protects it from the desert heat. Sleeping also helps the squirrel to save energy so it needs less food to survive.

The meaning of dreams has always fascinated people. Five thousand years ago, in Mesopotamia, "seers" or "prophets" were studying dreams and giving their meanings.

Here are a few of the commonest dream themes and what psychologists usually say they mean:

- Flying — usually means you are feeling on top of the world.
- Falling — often means you are worried about failing an exam.
- Finding money — can mean you are full of confidence.

Midnight Feasts

A feast is a large, sumptuous celebration. A midnight feast is something you can enjoy with a friend or your family anytime. They don't have to be eaten at midnight, but they taste best after your normal bedtime.

You will need to plan and prepare your midnight feast during the day. Try a few of these:

Five-minute cake

You will need:
1/2 cup margarine (or butter)
1 heaped cup sugar
2 eggs
2 cups self-raising flour
1 tablespoon cocoa
2 tablespoons milk

How to make:
Grease a rectangular cake tin and put to one side.
Cream margarine and sugar, then add eggs. Sift flour and cocoa and fold into mixture, adding milk gradually.
This should take 5 minutes.
Pour into cake tin. Cook in moderate oven for 30 minutes.

Fairy bread

You will need:
thinly sliced bread
butter
nonpareils (100s and 1000s)

How to make:
Cut the crusts off the bread, butter generously.
Sprinkle plenty of nonpareils onto the bread. Eat.

Hot chocolate drink

You will need:
vacuum flask
cup for each person
1 cup milk for each person
1 teaspoon sugar for each cup
1 teaspoon cocoa for each cup

How to make:
Heat the vacuum flask with hot water.
Warm the milk, either in a saucepan on the stove or in a jug in the microwave oven.
Add cocoa and sugar. Carefully pour into vacum flask.

Cold drinks

You can use the vacuum flask for cold drinks like fruit juice or lemonade.

Frankfurters

You will need:
   vacuum flask
   1 frankfurter for each person
   1 bread roll each person
   butter
   tomato ketchup

How to make:
   Heat vacuum flask as for hot chocolate drink.
   Place frankfurters in saucepan and bring to boil, then simmer for two minutes. When ready, slip frankfurters into vacuum flask.
   Slit open one side of each roll and butter. Wrap in foil. Borrow the bottle of tomato ketchup.
   When ready to start your feast, tip frankfurters out of flask, place in roll, add sauce and enjoy.

Coconut ice

You will need:
   1/4 cup cream cheese
   3 cups icing sugar
   1/2 cup desiccated coconut
   1/4 teaspoon vanilla essence
   red food colouring

How to make:
   Grease a flat cake tin and put to one side.
   Beat cream cheese and gradually add icing sugar, coconut and vanilla. Stir or knead till smooth.
   Place half the mixture in the cake tin. Colour the other half with the food colouring and spread over the first half.

Brain Teasers

Here are a few quiet games that won't disturb everyone else in the house — only your brain will be working.

What's it made of?

This is a game for two or more players. Everyone sits on the bed with a pencil and paper. The players are allowed five minutes to list all the things in the bedroom made from wood. When this game is finished, start another, this time list all the things made from plastic. And so on. Suggested categories are: cotton, metal, fabric, paper. If in doubt ask an adult to judge.

How many?

For this game you will need a pencil and paper each, plus the telephone book. The aim is to guess, as near as possible, the number of people whose name is North. Each player makes a guess, then you open the telephone book and count. The nearest correct answer is the winner. Next guess how many people are called South or East or West. If you live in a big city and decide to try and guess how many are called Smith or Jones, then you are likely to take hours to finish the game.

Pelmanism

Two or more can play this memory game and all you need is a pack of cards. The aim is to collect the most pairs. Sit on the floor. One player shuffles the cards, then places them at random, face down, on the floor. When all the cards are laid out each player takes a turn to turn over two cards. Everyone must see what the cards are and remember where they are. If it is a pair, or if you can make up a pair by remembering where a matching card is, then the player keeps the pair. If they don't match, then the cards are turned face down again IN THE SAME PLACE — this is important. The winner is the player who has collected the most pairs.

Clock patience

Here is a game you can play alone — all you need is a pack of cards and a clear space. Shuffle the cards, now set them out in a circle as if you are marking off the numbers on a clock face, from 1 around to 12. The 13th card is placed in the centre of the clock (as shown). All cards must be placed face down. Use up the whole pack of cards going round the clock, plus the one in the centre, in order. You will finish up with four cards on each pile. The final card you put down will be in the centre and is turned face up.

The object of this game is to end up with all the cards in their correct place, face up, around your clock. To do this you take the card that you turned up in the centre, which may have been a 2, and place it under the 2 pile on the clock. Then you turn the top card on that pile up and place that card in its right place. And so on until all the cards are face up and all are in the right place.

Here's how your cards work as numbers:

$$
\begin{aligned}
\text{An ace} &= 1 \\
2 &= 2 \\
3 &= 3 \\
4 &= 4 \\
5 &= 5 \\
6 &= 6 \\
7 &= 7 \\
8 &= 8 \\
9 &= 9 \\
10 &= 10 \\
\text{a jack} &= 11 \\
\text{a queen} &= 12 \\
\text{a king} &= \text{centre of clock.}
\end{aligned}
$$

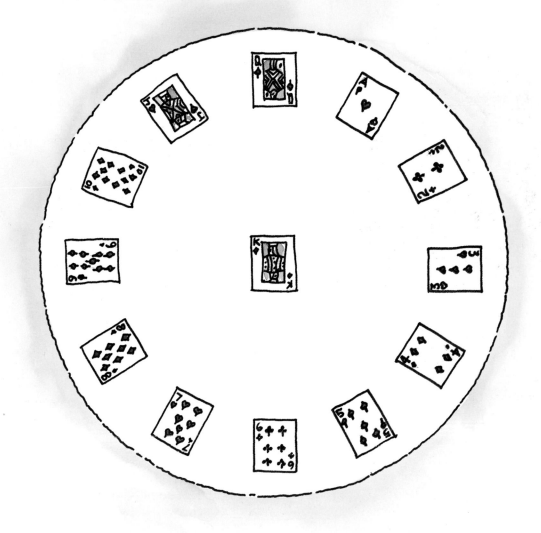

Painless Beds

There are times when you, or a member of your family, will have to spend a day or two in bed. There is nothing worse than being uncomfortable when you're not feeling well, so try these few practical hints to brighten up a stay in bed.

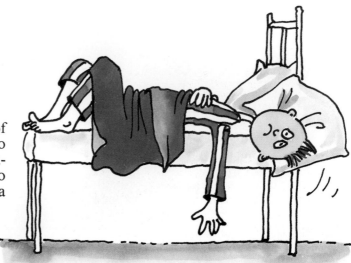

Footrest

This is a great way to stop you slipping down to the bottom of the bed.

You will need one single bed sheet and one pillow. Wrap the pillow up in the middle of the sheet, twisting the sides of the sheet to hold the pillow firm. Place in the bed to support feet, tuck the sheets in tightly.

Comfortable pillows

This makes the pillows comfortable and gives support in the right places.

You will need five pillows. Put one at the bottom, then angle two pillows together longways (as shown). The fourth pillow goes across these two behind the middle of where the back will rest. The last pillow on top for the head.

Bedside table

Use a small table, or the seat of a chair, placed near the head of the bed. This holds books, a glass of water and a food tray.

Continental quilts

These are much lighter than blankets and trap the air around the body. The ones filled with down feathers are warmer than the synthetic. The quilt folds into the curves of the sleeper, trapping a warm layer of air next to the body.

Continental quilts should be at least 30 cm wider than the bed. Do not put anything like blankets or a bedspread on top as this will squash out the air and reduce the warmth. Remember to shake your quilt frequently so the feathers are evenly distributed.

Cellular blankets

Woollen or cotton cellular blankets also provide warmth without weight. If you are extra cold, wrap yourself in one of these blankets.

These blankets are also very useful if you go camping in cold weather. You wrap yourself in one then crawl into your sleeping bag.

Mitred corners

When making up a bed for someone who is going to be there all day, be sure you have the corners looking neat and tidy. Here's how to do it:

1 Tuck in the bottom sheet at the ends of the bed. Pick up the edge of the sheet, about 45 cm back from the corner of the mattress. Take the piece that is hanging down and tuck in firmly.

2 Now bring down the piece of sheet you have been holding.

3 Tuck firmly in. Then you'll have a neat and tidy corner. Do all four corners the same way.

Body Fun

Here are a few exercises that can be done in your bedroom. Some you can do alone, others you'll need a partner, all will help you keep fit.

Caterpillar walk

From a standing position bend forward and touch your toes. Walk your hands away from you, as far as they will go. Now, walk your feet up to meet your hands. Do this several times.

Bicycling

Lying flat on your back, lift your legs from the hips. Now pretend you are riding a bicycle in the air.

Rowing on land

Sit on the floor facing your partner, with knees bent and holding hands. One of you lies back, keeping your knees bent, while the other stands up with body bent forward. Now change positions and don't let go of hands.

Lunging to war

Stand up, feet together. Put your left foot forward, knee bent, at the same time swing your left arm forward to imitate a sword thrust. Recover to standing position and repeat with right foot and arm.

Coffee grinder

Stand up, feet apart, facing your partner. Grasp hands. Swing your arms from side to side keeping them as straight as possible.

Sawing wood

Sit down, legs crossed, facing your partner. Grasp hands. Alternately bend and straighten your arms as if you are sawing up wood. Sometimes you can pretend that the saw is stuck — this means that one of you will hold while the other pulls.

Wheelbarrow

The wheelbarrow lies on the floor, face down with legs apart. The driver picks up the legs, at about the knees. The wheelbarrow now rises up on the hands and begins to walk, while the driver pushes. The wheelbarrow can pretend to be carrying a heavy load and resist the driver.

Surviving Going to Bed

Going to bed doesn't have to be a problem. It is the ideal time to catch up on things you never have time to do during the day, like some of these:

Day dreaming

All you need to do is lie back in bed, make yourself comfortable and close your eyes. Now you can let your thoughts wander — you can imagine things, make up stories, plan what you will do tomorrow or remember things you did today. It's very relaxing.

reef knot

clove hitch

figure eight knot

Practise knotting

Lying in bed is the ideal time to practise all those knots you need to know when you go camping, boating or hiking. Take a length of rope (not string) to bed and try these:

reef knot
clove hitch
figure eight knot
bowline

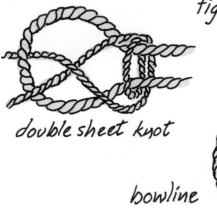

double sheet knot

bowline

Reading

Bed must be one of the best places in the world to enjoy a good book. If you have to turn your light out right in the middle of an exciting spot, you can always read for a few more minutes by hiding under the bed covers and using a torch, or one of those little battery lights that clips on to the top of the book. Remember, don't do this for longer than ten minutes — it's bad for your eyes.

Turn on the Walkman

Listening to music or stories on tape or using a Walkman is very relaxing, and you won't be disturbing anyone else. Remember to choose your tapes before going up to bed, then settle back and enjoy them. You can always read while listening to music.

Writing letters

Sit up in bed with something solid on your lap, like a tray, to rest your postcards or writing pad on. Now you can catch up on all your letters to pen pals and family.

ZZzzzzzz......

Now it is time to settle down and turn out the light. Put everything away, straighten your bed, make sure you have enough warm covers. If you are feeling wide awake, ask an adult to make you a warm drink (not tea or coffee) — it will help you to relax and sleep.

GOODNIGHT — SLEEP TIGHT — MIND THE BEDBUGS DON'T BITE!